this wonderful perpetual beautiful

stephen roxborough

NeoPoiesis Press

ℛ

NeoPoesisPress.com

Stephen Roxborough – this wonderful perpetual beautiful
ISBN 978-0-9832747-1-1 (paperback: alk. paper)
    1. Poetry. I   Roxborough, Stephen

Printed in the United States of America

First Edition

Cover, design and typography: Milo Duffin and Stephen Roxborough

contents

I: the size of sky

2: when the great green explodes

3: all my spiritual mistakes

4: the sunset of the sunset

1

the size of sky

tonight cannot be measured
might be too much
to know

this wonderful perpetual beautiful

spiral
fractal
molecular
dissolve
out of others
into ourselves
and then
other others
the engine
of universal flow
the wave
that tumbles
mountains
into sand
takes planets
to pieces
collapses stars
and shreds
everything
we think we know
into everything
we don't
as fuel
to keep going
creating
and fading
into and through
this wonderful
perpetual
beautiful
spiral
fractal
molecular
dissolve

accordingly

everyone will be wise
in the future everyone will be sensible
wear sensible shoes and act accordingly
in the future
wise action according to everyone will be the act
of the future everyone will be futuristic someday
according to god according to everyone
and their shoes
in the future everyone will be godless and free
act accordingly in the future or else
play accordions wisely in your godless future
in the future accordions will play themselves

act three in the future: there will be
no accordions
everyone will get nostalgic for the accordion god
and act as if they were wise in the future
everyone will be according to god
in the future everyone will not act accordingly
wisdom is unholy in the future
to act accordingly is to stay out of trouble
in the future jails will be bigger and much better
everyone will need some punishment
in the future
thinking of accordions will be a crime

lawrence welk is a revolutionary in the future
to act accordingly is to act with wisdom
everyone will act as one in the future
accordingly for everyone to act
in the future everyone will be discredited
everyone must act now to avoid the future
be wise and don't act accordingly
play accordions in the street the future cannot
wait for wisdom and forced accord
one chord might save the future

the morning mirror

the only moment
of daily truth

sometimes he sees a dashing
old fool
other days
just an old fool

but he looks every morning
just the same

thinks perhaps if
he didn't look everyday
his age would sneak
up on him

puts down the razor

this frightening twilight
of time is sneaky

relentless

master student

the boy keeps a little box
of ideas
just in case

carries them everywhere
keeps it close
so close
no one ever gets to hold it
or peek inside

secretly
he confides to me
the box is really completely
empty

except teacher
believes the box is full
of great ideas
full of uncontainable
bliss

think like an engineer

what is the most efficient means
to carry your sorrow around?

how much abuse can you internalize
before impacting domestic integrity?

are corrupted relationship files
worth salvaging and saving?

how much tension is diffused
by giving way?

why do mood drugs enhance the moment
but steal joy in the long run?

is deflection an effective mode
of emotional armor?

can sustained practice of letting go
bring people in conflict together?

how is the mantra "only always now"
more powerful than a locomotive?

impact of linear vs. non-linear time
on family structure and stability?

what constant vibration is optimum
for health and pleasure?

bathroom meditation

cat stretch bed let thought go
downward facing dog let thought go
wipe sleep world let thought go
let thought go

shit shower shave let thought go
pluck comb brush let thought go
wash rinse dry let thought go
let thought go

flush squeeze brush let thought go
lather soap shampoo let thought go
twist turn sit let thought go
let thought go

stand gaze gawk let thought go
smile frown reach let thought go
bend towel blow let thought go
let thought go

pick floss pee let thought go
wipe fog groan let thought go
creak stretch squat let thought go
let thought go

judge push scrape let thought go
touch smooth flush let thought go
shit shower shave let thought go
let thought go

basic used to be black

today basic comes
in a rainbow assortment
of styles and colors

one to suit your every mood
one for each day
of your life

they say if you want
something different
you'd have to live 842 years
to repeat the same basic
twice

but with more choice
comes more responsibility
and basic becomes
an albatross
that peacock struts
around your neck

the simple life
much more than you thought
much less than you
expected

those perfect days

when your hands turn to stone
and your shoes are filled
with lead

when your bank account is dry
and all your bills arrive
in the same mailbox

when the neighbor collects
that favor to punch you
in the mouth

when your only car won't start
and the vultures circle
overhead

oh those endless perfect
sunny days when everything
goes wrong

the quest

some seek fame others
fortune some just
need to follow
desire

yet some only want to be left
alone
with their craft

find out
if
they can stop time
or learn to
fly
without wings

to ease the madness
and exchange molecules
of joy

but always
without expectation

hope

or the petty
burdens of fashion

and boss

how much to suffer for your

art before the art suffers before the artist
dies before enough time passes and no one cares
the revolution is over post post post
modernism museums crumble
that war that culture that medium dead
gone forgotten
even the concept of suffering
forgotten

what is a piece of an ear worth
the price of a shriveled liver
thousands of bottles but was it the good stuff
or rot gut
at what price time and fashion
when the pills become cheaper stronger
faster higher
over the counter or under the table
new research shows suffering will save us
and the fashion will be for more
excellent pain
and beautiful suffering

bad air bad water bad food bad religion
bad love bad laws bad leaders bad economy
and suffering will become
the highest art
how much are you willing to suffer
for your country for your art
how much will your bank
account suffer
your children suffer
suffering children is an art

or will you rebel
avoid the natural attraction to suffering
reinvent happiness without a pill
create some new flavor
of the month every week
bubblegum ice cream
is the new suffering

how much can you afford
to suffer for art

oral fixation

the scores of things
we put to our lips

many more
than we'd care
to admit

those that nourish
those that tempt
and those that attempt
both

never enough
to stop trying more

yet of all things
we crave and taste
how few will fully satisfy

how few will
kiss us back

the sky he contemplates this evening

may not be the one he thinks
he sees

hard to tell in this light

the size of sky
tonight cannot be measured
might be too much
to know

the clouds change too fast
to recognize them

the sun drops like a god in the ocean

his mind cannot keep up
with his eyes
his eyes reflect the fire in the sky
he rubs them and the fire
spreads to his hands
and whatever he touches
catches fire

his world engulfed in flames

everything bends and waves in heat
sucking atmosphere
and melting landscape
until the pinks and purples
filter through

and day heals itself
with night

advice

no matter how drunk or tired
you should always remember to brush
floss
and take off
all your street clothes
before going to bed

well maybe not take off
your clothes
because that can be a lot of work
too early or too late
in the morning

but never forget to brush and floss
if you have any floss
otherwise
a good brushing will do
unless you can't find
a toothbrush
then simply finding
the bed
is a good job

although i often find
the floor
a reasonable
substitute

your body will tell you when

it needs more rest
and it's your job to listen

slow down
drink water
go to bed early
sleep late
don't worry
laugh more
relax with a book
everything else
can wait

except effortlessness
and letting go

cut the strings
of those things hanging
over your head

clear your mind
of deadlines

listen to the rain
learn to use gravity

understand
how falling is sometimes
the best
we can do

lesson #83

there's nowhere to go
and no place
to hide

shoes on shoes off

everything is alive
yet everything
must die

shoes on shoes off

love is not a science
love is an approximation
of eternity

shoes on shoes off

nothing lasts forever
nothing
but nothing and change

shoes on shoes off

they said he died with
his boots on
but he never wore boots

shoes on shoes off

we fill up at the mountain
and empty into ocean
shoes on shoes off

what to do

when you run out of yourself
you'll know what you're made of

when you run out of yourself
is not the time to order more

when you run out of yourself
your life walks into you

when you run out of yourself
there's no one to become

when you run out of yourself
fill up on emptiness

when you run out of yourself
time to stop running

an understanding

over the years
i've come to understand
i hate you
is the same as
i love you

but with more edge

even though love
and hate seem to be opposites
they are really
married to each other
both trying to get a divorce
but complications
always arise

love has charm and allure
while hate has desire
and rage

together
a dangerous velcro
that keeps the attraction
going

hell
it keeps
the species going

no one can figure out
exactly why

he grew comfortable with

himself in old age
less critical of his imperfections
embraced each new ache
with wonder

became kinder to his dark side
gave more compassion
to his feet
made peace with his hands
began to laugh at
his reflection

talked to himself like
an old friend
or a young child
offered himself all kinds
of good advice

once he surprised himself
with an expensive
gift
something only he knew
he wanted

he decided growing old
with himself
agreed with him
and he figured on doing it
for as long as he
could

she had only eight minutes to live

and all she could think of
was eyebrows

every eyebrow she'd ever known

were they plucked
trimmed or free range? did they
furrow?

vegetarian or vegan?
worry about the economy?
support the troops?

were they trained at birth
or brainwashed over time? everyone had
eyebrows
but nobody seemed to admit it

thought when was the last time you struck up
a conversation about eyebrows?

the media virtually ignores them

was it a conspiracy
and who was behind it?

the last minute of her life
she made peace
with her eyebrows

experienced overwhelming compassion
for all the eyebrows in the world

couch floating

you know you're ready
more than ready
when it's time to let go
of the ments:
achievement punishment
requirement accomplishment
advancement payment
judgment and attainment

when you reach the end of fragment
all the slicing and dicing yourself
in 5,000 directions
when it's time to pink slip time
let the clouds in your head
waft by and disperse
let the whole world
come to you for a change

let go of low vibration
all earth binding tethers
of want and worry
let your thoughts wash over
rinse evaporate
let your body dissolve
into atomic cosmos
let everything melt into itself

everything but the couch
hovering in a room
without walls floor or ceiling
everything simply being and not being
on a planet drifting in space
and you find yourself
lighter than care

the final act

before and after
death is all
we know

the guest that never leaves
the endless nagging
cough
the only thing
you can count on

death gives shape and meaning
to existence

without death we could
not live
wouldn't know
how to

because death is the good guy
the only one who can
save your life

in the end

instant reincarnation

she never wanted the book to end
so she read it again and again and again

she never wanted the movie to end
so she watched it again and again and again

she never wanted her song to end
so she played it again and again and again

she never wanted her life to end
so she gave birth again and again and again

she never wanted her love to end
so she fell in love again and again and again

she never wanted the good times to end
but they never ever really began

until she stopped all her wanting
again and again and again and again

2

when the great green explodes

there's hell to pay but we tell
ourselves the pain
is worth it

freezing frames

snap shot eyelash
shutter stutter crackle flash

fisheye redeye mind's eye
all seeing eye
all in favor
say aye

with ultra powerful depth
of stealing souls field

copy capture
picture faker
image maker
symbol taker

icon nikon digital pixel
mega zoom blow up tycoon

pop bulb flash snap
instant paparazzi
pop! pop!
art

a traffic jam is more like stew

than something sweet
to spread on morning toast

we don't jam in traffic
we stew
in our hundreds of tons of plastic
steel and glass coffins
all spewing deadly fumes

half of us fuming ourselves
frustrated with our lives
jobs relationships families friends
mothers fathers
offspring
credit cards mortgage

it doesn't matter how much
you stir the pot
it's the same old stew

and we're all in it
together
all driving alone
and sifting in
a plantation of refined sugar
won't ever

make it a jam

used to be paradise but

now it's all eden
after they divided the garden
into plots and subplots
enough for ten novels

two gates and six guards
four designs and three colors
a man's home is his castle
surround by a moat
of your own kind

good schools for your offspring
good stores for your shopping
good sprinkler systems
for your immaculate lawn

friendly policeman patrolled
safe and secure gang free
clean happy streets
slow down
perfect children at play

the man-made lake
with a dozen swans preening
their clipped wings
under a rainbow geyser
looks so natural

the old farm is a golf course
with an invitation to join
the new country club
called purgatory

hero sandwich

non-stop war with a side
of home fries or potato chips
your choice
hold the onions
substitute deficit spending
and a new fighter jet
with cost over-runs
and extra mayo lettuce tomato
politics and pickle
in the middle
pour on the mustard gas
disability insurance
two slices of real cheddar cheese
a dozen or more videogenic
multi-star generals
hundreds of thousands of boots
on the ground pepper
thousands of medium rare
purple hearts
sick valentines for the dead
and the perfect can't let
the families
of the fallen down
no exit strategy
lovingly stacked between
puppet government
and good old fashioned
nation building
all on a 100% bleached
treasure enriched
toasted sesame seed
buns yum

most of the past is undistinguished

unwanted discarded rejected
as trivial unworthy
insignificant
minor unheroic
ordinary

yet these moments
are the building blocks of greatness
and infamy

hitler during toilet training
when mao learned to tie
his shoes
the first time jesus hit
his thumb with a hammer
when moses was caught smoking
behind a bush
and the time young
george washington almost choked
on a cherry pit

all the details of the unknown
forgotten secrets
of history

my father's generation never

knew themselves
growing up in the great depression
they were brainwashed
into believing
a steady job with steady pay
is the path to happiness

but then they were shipped off
to war

when they came back
they didn't talk about it
how they saved us
from all the madmen dictators
at least most of them
they just came home
and went back
to work
back to simple
nine to five

supported the family
drank their booze
read the paper
kissed the wife good morning
kissed the wife good night
church on sunday
and returned
to the ordinary grind
on monday

over and over and over
and because they didn't know themselves
they didn't really know
their kids

that's how the 60s were born

whatever happened

whatever happened to all the golden boys?
the millions of all-americans
our sports heroes
our high school scholars
our bouncy bubbly vivacious
cheerleaders leading us on
leading us one by one
to the promised land

our flawless skin prom queens
who can't pronouce environmental
and don't want to

our pray for world peace beauty contest
disasters

our endless supply of talented
beautiful strong intelligent
military fodder

whatever happened
to generation after generation
of unlimited brilliance

faded into landscape
zapped of zeal and spark
folded into the system
left all alone

the twinkle gone

no more war old age and disease

no more hangovers early mornings
foolish work irksome noises
bad manners ignorance vile drivers
poverty and sleepless nights

no more mediocrity hunger dirty water
atomic bombs terrorism bad cops
mosquitoes missionary christians
wrong numbers and rubber checks

no more poisonous snakes politicians
bad teachers violence gaining weight
bosses toothaches donuts heartaches
lying cheating and relentless headaches

no more weak flavorless fruity beer
bad wallpaper indulgent poems
middle men self-righteous religion
dark days and paint by numbers

no how no way none of the above
cancel purge delete done gone pause
yet how would we know when
happiness slapped us in the face

the human race

we think we're a race
we call it a race

no start no finish no winners
no one arrives on time

they arrive in place
on the path

many destinations
no where to go

arrive by leaving
leave by arriving

get there
by being still

normality is another kind of insanity

white men like to chop down trees
live to kill whatever they please
try to bring nature to her knees
white men like to chop down trees

white men like to mow the grass
chop chop lawn sittin on ass
cuttin down green and burnin gas
white men like to mow the grass

white men like to spray their weeds
chemical solutions are friends indeed
kill at will and then they bleed
into lakes to make stronger weeds

white men assume they have control
but cuttin and killin takes its toll
just when you think you're on a roll
nature looms to swallow us whole

white men like to chop down trees
white men like to mow the grass
white men like to spray their weeds
white men assume they have control

when the great green explodes

i'll be in that number
carrying my banner lifting it higher
no more war on whatever
they're selling
when the great green explodes
smell the carnage and taste rotting logos
as they melt
on my raging red tongue
when the great green explodes
there's hell to pay but we tell
ourselves the pain
is worth it
when the great green explodes
banding together when falling apart
no sour political grapes
flashpoint tip of the melting
relationship iceberg
when the great green explodes
i'll be in that number
waving to the passive oppressed
by youth and beauty
driving my flintstone car
dreaming of the jetsons
or jeannie or freedom
for burma shamrock isle and tibet
when the great green explodes
billions of jellyfish moons
shine over
the hungry planet
guide on fire for change
when the great green explodes
lips kissing spiritual flames
into the bright night
into the dark days ahead
into our waking dream
open flowers all
when the great green explodes

he found himself talking to franz kafka

a long lost friend from another time
they sat in his bedroom
and ecstatically
discussed the old coffeehouses
of prague

the quality of their brew
the efficiency of service
the friendliness of the waiters
the ambience of the rooms
whether the space was best to read
write or dream in
the beauty of the female clientele
the distinct way each woman
held their cup
and completely from memory
the exact dimensions
of their lips

together they meticulously
catalogued the lips
face by face place by place
all the beautiful full medium narrow
upturned pouty lipped women
in urban bohemia

the list became an underground sensation
eventually its reputation
grew and the book of voluptuous
lip descriptions
was deemed too erotic
for the masses
and confiscated by authorities

one morning upon awakening
kafka was gone
yet he discovered
he'd been sentenced to 20 years
hard labor
in another less
imaginative poem

on a modest hill overlooking the past

a wide porch supports a row
of creaking
antique rockers
bobbing back and forth
slowly sawing
the chains of time

they want to take off and return
to the mirth
of weightless youth
as thoughts
and talk about what was
embellished

by what might have been
dot evening sky
like glowing clouds
passing from another age
ready to fade to the other side
of twilight

the original version

seemed plausible to most
until all the facts
came in
or what they told us were facts
and then denied them
buried them
discredited them
because they didn't quite fit
with the original version
which later became
the official version
the one we
saw heard read on the nonstop news
hour after hour
day after day
night after night
until it became old hat
and the facts quietly faded
put to bed like so many
unruly children
so we could all sleep better
at night knowing
the truth would not
terrorize us

knowledge is a burden

in this age of information
you cannot remember
what you had for breakfast
the current president
what year it is
friends and famous faces
how many children you have
or what you did two minutes ago

you know there are great holes
in your head where a college
of hippocampus once
flourished
enormous multi-storied structures
housing thousands of rooms
protecting billions
of files now stamped
"access denied"

whole cities inside you crumble
stacks of family encyclopedias erased
private civilizations destroyed
personal rosetta stones pulverized
facts figures stats records
data vanished
secret slates wiped clean
luggage lost baggage dropped

necessary preparation
for the next

words mean nothing

in isolation
out of context
without a language
just grunts
sounds

inarticulate
breaths of air

a letter on its own
gets even more
lonely

appears awkward
bizarre obtuse
groundless
unwarranted

without writers

too many old lonely
letters
living on their own
eating alphabet
blah blah

struggling
to make ends meet

danger: lost language ahead

every 14 days a language
is lost forever
gone

no tongue left to remember
how to speak
specific knowledge
unique stories
rare wisdom never
to pass this way again

gone
in a heartbeat
translations never made
or even possible
gone

extinct at a rate faster
than birds mammals plants
gone

20% of the planet's
distinct 7,000 languages
in danger
gone

quick!
grab that recorder
save another mother tongue
besides english
money or
war

or is that
the same language?

must be spring

all the poets are turning
their dirt
plowing words
exposing pink worms
fresh hurt
and dark deep
secrets

these open wounds
make way for rare seed
new poem sprouts
for ardor
to take root
grab hold of firm
holy ground

nourish inward
then branch outward
blindly reach for
some unbroken sky
and kiss
the summer sun
one more time

when someone says i love you and means it

their hair beard and fingernails grow faster
their sense of humor and universe expands
policemen smile at them their sub-atomic
vibration flows at a higher frequency result-
ing in weight loss more laughter heightened
intuition and appetite suppressant a career in
the military is less likely poetic inhibitions
are reduced short flights of fancy likely the
weather improves small irritations disappear
shades of pink and green glow around them
their shoes stop squeaking trees begin to talk
to them invitations to dinner parties multiply
exponentially cats purr around them bowel
movements become effortless their dreams
more vivid less disturbing sleep comes easily
less is needed news does not distract know-
ledge loses power the future less important
investments appear ludicrous lips swell eyes
dilate throat chakras open creative powers
return play defeats work circulation improves
their life force is strong and undemanding

meaningful beauty

for softer smoother
tighter thinner leaner longer
stronger more radiant
charming charismatic wavelength
plus safe soothing superb
insightful vibration

try our secret exclusive
100% pure natural organic special
non-polluting fraud
and creature free meditation
with regular daily use
meaningful beauty

will diminish signs of inner revulsion
and reduce nagging symptoms
of outer repugnance
while completely transforming
every aspect of your wretched weak
browbeaten existence

for optimal results
empty mind thoroughly
and do not i repeat
do not succumb to cosmetic surgery
obsessive navel gazing
and/or non-essential products

on world's edge

the bondi caveman props up feet
on discarded stool and relaxes
in his cliffside easy chair

watches the wheels from on high
soaks in the beachfront panorama
lesser men sell their lives to possess

he's camped here with books paintings
pots pans and one comfortable chair
for the last seven years

friend to surfers and seagulls he recites
poetry and protects the possessions
of ocean swimmers

mystic guardian of word and beach
sage inspiration or obvious eyesore
jhyimy wears two hats at once

one for the bloody rule makers
and one for freedom from the grind
of the ceaseless machine

the collector

traveled throughout asia
from bali to tibet
accumulating buddhas
cast and carved
to schlep them in backpack
from town to village
and village
to town in search
of more burdensome icons
to weigh him further
down
make each step
of this material quest
more arduous
a test of will between
desire
and the stones
who whisper sanskrit chants
of non-attachment
and lightness
of being

many theories but

no certain answers
no pictures
no proof no positive identification
no reception no connection
to your bloodline
no face in the mirror
no mail no letters no words
no sentence no punctuation no
trace of DNA
no severed toes or ears
no footprint no fingerprints
no newsprint no witness
no one at the scene no
intelligent questions
no breaking news no scent
no focus no sound no vision
no clue no deductions no real sherlock holmes
no imagination no location
no intersection no crossroads
no meaning no dots
no numbers to crunch
no real time
everything happens at once
but nothing happens
not now no thread
no body no taste cold case
no color no contrast
no horizontal hold
no strings no rope no emotion
no attachment
not even you anymore
only love and dreams of better angels
it will always be this way

how to find god

blow a dandelion
eat a sunset
look under the welcome mat
become a sky watcher
watch children play
taste a fresh strawberry
soar with eagles
dive with dolphins
die and live again
open a door for a stranger
shine your shoes
lose a quarter in a slot machine
change a diaper
inhale the moment
walk around the block
bet the cubs to win the series
listen to mozart
body surf
pull a weed
count grains of sand on a beach
meditate on emptiness
stop the bleeding
glorify peace
teach someone to overcome fear
watch bob beaman after his mexico jump
cradle a tarantula in your hand
let go of the pain
let go of the pleasure
make love with every breath
smile
return a smile
give way
write a long letter
practice balance
fast

close your eyes and listen
be there for someone
give
look for anything
become everything
make love make love
make love!

the gravity of forgiveness

there's a fine line between good and evil
love and hate freedom and prison
war and peace darkness and light
guinness and corona low fat and fat free
free tibet and sugar-free fortune cookies but
sometimes the line blurs and doubles or triples
i can't see it clearly or it fades transparent
and i do the wrong thing like yell
QUIET! at the kids
or stumble in the dark drive home drunk
avoid piercing daylight with cheap sunglasses
take a nap on the couch instead of
cleaning the toilets
or make a slow comma at a red stop sign
wash new colors with old whites
drive ten miles an hour over the speed limit
or i buy plastic doo-dads made in chinese prisons
because they're less than half the price
of the whim-whams
made in the USA by hard-working illegal aliens
but then the payback blows our way
and my clear blue
suburban pseudo industrial-free western skies
are shanghaied by three-day-old far east pollution
or i forget common sense logic and don't
buy organic
instead get the genetic-engineered
extra-pesticide flavor
antibiotic-laden bovine growth hormone
enriched and bleached full-fat variety
of inscrutable
oriental dressing or ice cream or sour cream
or heavy whipping cream
then thinking of whipping i feel as guilty
as a fallen priest confessing to

an unclean cardinal
that i want to be punished a little like tobacco tax
with twenty soft lashes to my wallet
or perhaps one tongue lashing
from a surgeon general warning
meant for the unborn and smoking pregnant
so i don't feel too irresponsible
but then a burning flag somewhere on TV
reminds me i live in america! damn it
land of the free and home of aspartame
where no one will sue me for
below-average consumer ignorance
because there are no laws
against the imperfect choices of
supply and demand
and i am so very very sorry for sinking
instead of rising
and falling oh so short
of myself

lazy drizzle

soft raindrops are blue
the color of heaven
and tears
the hue of all my
forgiveness

soft raindrops are blue
the gentle gurgle
of drowning
the echo of forgotten
laughter

soft raindrops are blue
on october sunday
mornings
the faint purr
of dream-state snoring

soft raindrops are blue
a perfect orange cloud floats closer
while black coffee
waits
for a cup

soft raindrops are blue
a mute chorus of clowns
sings and gives
themselves
to the ground

3

all my spiritual mistakes

the perfection of your music
frightened me
scares me even still

they nailed a little christ

on my wall
next to my bed
and he hung there
on the cross
hanging on my wall
expressionless
changeless

all shiny golden
dying all over again
dying every damn day
suffocated in gold
and nailed to wood
that miraculously turned to
plastic

high grade plastic
with imitation wood grain

trophy gold-plated jesus lead
on high grade plastic on yellow latex
on drywall
nailed to real wood
holding up the roof to keep us
dry and warm

while i rest
and heal in bed

he never moved
never ever spoke
but i knew
by the look in his eyes
he'd rather be
somewhere else

the sound of one hand clapping

many years ago
maybe a few decades ago
the hands of time
used to pat me on the back
encourage me to
keep going

inch forward they'd say
follow your dreams
keep it up
be somebody
and even look forward

now each hour
slaps me in the face
punches me in the gut
uses sign language
to tell me
you ain't what you used to be
you're going nowhere fast

out of the way old man

and each midnight
every clock in every town
looks like
it's giving me
the proverbial finger

the learning curve

too steep
the merry-go-round square
the wheel of fortune steals your money
the fun house feels
like hell
the mirrors melt your face
the ferris wheel
grinds you into dust
the cotton candy gives you
cancer
the carnies bark three balls
for your soul
the lemonade makes you thirsty
the faces all strange
the girls have long beards
the tattoo man becomes
your wife
and i'm stuck
on the tilt-a-whirl
waiting
for the weekend

the first time i held

a cherry bomb in my hands
was like the first time i kissed
a girl
only better
i mean my mother
wouldn't have approved
of either

both tight and hard
but the bomb was
perfect

all it needed was a match
and somewhere
to go

it didn't have any feelings
and didn't want any

single-minded

one purpose one
direction
yet the excitement
of holding it

while the fuse burned dangerous
anticipation

inevitable

i sit in my office and stare

at a blank document
on my computer
wondering what's next
when my 12-year old wanders in
asks
how come you work
so hard
and never make
any money?

he leaves before i can formulate
an answer about poetry
and money
how most of the time
they never meet
not even halfway and if they ever do
never long enough to become
close friends

but now i want to tell him how
the best things in life
are labors of love
not work

how poetry may look
like work
but feels to me like
breathing

now the page is mostly full
and i have enough
air

to go on living

are you talking to me?

i've been in the bathroom for the last
ten minutes
and didn't hear a word

are you talking to me?

i'm washing the dishes
and the faucet is a waterfall
of white noise
that drowns you out

are you talking to me?

the TV is on and i'm watching
my favorite reality show
and surprise
you're not in it!

are you talking to me?

i'm on the phone to my sister
and whatever you said
well i can't listen
to two blah blah people at once

are you talking to me?

i mean i saw your lips move but
didn't notice any words coming out
maybe i was daydreaming
or listening
to something better

are you talking to me?

i'm downstairs to get
out of your way
and you sound like you're mumbling
into a paper bag

are you talking to me?

i'm busy grinding coffee beans
so you can wake up
with a fresh cup
but i guess your tongue
never sleeps

are you talking to me?

because i'm tired she said
without any words
to fall asleep to

of all my spiritual mistakes

you are the hardest
to play

your instrument
too beautiful
dates me
intimidates me ruins me
makes me crave
you more

god knows i prayed
for all unseemly things

physical pleasures
impermanent highs
driven by flesh
and bone

always another taste
of earthly indulgence
inside your holy
temple

forbidden fruit with divine juice
from whom all damnation
and blessings flow

the perfection of your music
frightened me
scares me even still
triggers me
to always strike
the wrong
chord

her voice flies through me

willingly
resonates in places
other sounds
can't reach

trips all my triggers
flips every switch
trembles warbles quivers shudders
shivers pulsates
a great cosmic buzz

opens all my rusted gates
cracks my secret safe
picks the lock
on my private chapel
and waltzes right in

my steely interior turns to mush
my blood pumps backwards
my moral backbone sags
and breaks
into a wet paper bag
of scrambled brain cells

all because of the lovely lilt
of her accent
the perfect pitch
the beautiful reverb tumble
the dazzling color
her vivid timbre
the constant harmonic flow
of her holy chords
the joyful glaswegian gypsy way
she beats her sacred
vibration

on my inner drum

morning meditation

she didn't know where to walk
when the grass beneath her feet quietly
froze from the dew

each blade a tiny green icicle
crunching
and crumbling
under every giant stride

her boot imprint enormous
in a lilliputian universe

not wanting to crush
a lowly bug
someone's broken egg child
crack spilt smashed
by boot tread

she noticed her lungs
bellowed vapor clouds of sound
across cozy sweet rotting
orange
pink autumn sky

realized she'd been standing
in the same spot for years

believed the stars
would soon return to help her
feel small again

the lepidoptress

she knows the secrets of butterflies
the eccentric code of their delicate etiquette
what they do in their spare time
what they really want to be
how hurricanes are born
memories of past lives
the magnitude of nectar reviews
their dragonfly nightmares
the seductive dance of flight
what breaks their weightless hearts
how many dog years in a butterfly second
if butterfly heaven exists
why a butterfly lie is the biggest
curl of the fingerprint tongue
how they attract the truest blues
esoteric scriptures on wings
favourite leaves of offspring
dizzying pheromones
flattering flower scents
and hot vacation spots

she knows the secrets of butterflies
hears their whispers
speaks with the same eyesight
touches the intense taste
of pure fleeting
smells their ecstasy
understands their disillusion
offers asylum in her palm

she knows the secrets of butterflies
and guards them
with her life

she listened to mongolian wind

caressing and whipping the steppes
softly whispering
hugging her chest and kissing
innocent cheeks
then in an instant
ferociously shouting
her down with piercing gusts
of desperate promise
exposing her senseless dreams
making her stare fearlessly inside herself
at the widest sky on earth
believe everything is impossible
and possible at the same time
grabs her by the collar
and shakes her with an edge
of sympathy
urging her to follow daring dreams
struggle survive and win
her freedom from loneliness
tender gentle breeze
of compassion
questions what will you add to the redundancy
of human incarnation
this holy camel clad profane vessel
imperfectly perfect
traversing ancient landscape
with all the baggage of a thousand past lives
trudging over hills so exhausted
tired of being trampled
worn down not out
she wishes she never came here
but now she needs
to return
she needs to hear more stories
from mongolian wind

she can see her reflection

in everyone's glasses
see herself much smaller
looking back
at herself
looking into a billion other people
with corrective lenses

understands for the first time
how alike
and superficial
we all are and wonders
how can all the optometrists
close their eyes at night

and pretend not to realize
this prescription
this reflective vision
this awakening this
revelation
can change the world

flowers

first she trims the ends
her sharpest knife
oblique cut
then arranges
in a hand blown vase
according to texture color length
composes a visual
symphony
adds cold water
waits about a week
for them to wilt
adds more water
waits for them to shivel
fade and fail
turn pale then brown
slowly effortlessly twist into themselves
become interesting
at last
rearranges them
loves them one more time
loves them even deeper
in decomposition
admires the beauty
of death

she stirs the curry

waits for potatoes to melt
into the sauce
the garlic and onions are patient
their flavors still bleeding
the gas flame is blue
and raging
cable news argues
in another room
the rice fluffed 30 minutes ago
the wine is almost out
of breath
but the potatoes
eyes gouged and heads
severed
feel empowered
and stubborn
her blade has given them
an edge
they refuse to fall apart
she feels
in her bones
they'd rather be
underground

she's in bed with another poet

deep undercovers
in the middle
of his love

kissing every line
stroking every stanza
moving to
the rhythm
of his breath
through her own

sucking the marrow
of his meaning

each thrust
of holy blood
on the sheets
takes her
deeper and deeper
into his pulse

a private place
where secret perfume
whispers
the church of word
into her

wanting ear

when your father

goes to the pool she said
he remembers
the past

doesn't know how to sign
his name
but something about walking
through the water
helps open his mind

he talks about you
calls you the swimmer

i was very hard on him he says
then starts to cry
and when i hear this
i think of all the workouts
and anger
all the roadtrips
and races
trying to beat
the clock

i begin to cry
pools tears

our last connection

whenever she starts with an apology

he knows he's in trouble
he knows he'll hear
her trademark

i love you...but

then the tide will turn
and soon the trickle becomes
a tirade of claims

blaming his behaviour

before he realizes it
he's defending himself against
trumped up charges

left wondering

how she fits a trojan horse
into an olive branch
and why he falls for it

every time

my world

in my world touch rhymes
with lonely he said

i'll take away your senses till you feel
no pain she said

blindness is another way of looking
at the world he said

you could say that about any of your
limitations she said

my world is full of emptiness
he said and she said

you've no idea how meaningless
fullness can be

his collective loneliness tonight

is tearing him apart
he's tuning in
the timeless ache of hank williams
the wounded depth of leonard cohen
and the fading whistle
of otis redding

surrounded by ghosts
who once needed a friend
with a full bottle of sympathy
or a lyric to lean on
and this crowd of forlorn
souls is both

dragging him down and lifting
him up when he realizes
this is the human condition
to want what doesn't ease the pain
to want what leads to more
of the same

in a relationship

he believes in a god
that doesn't know he exists

thinks the universe will be cancelled
due to lack of interest

he likes the smell of gasoline
and tangerines

savors small argentinean wines
in front of a dark fireplace

takes long walks
without you

life

he wished those curtains
were green

but they were decidedly red

yet when the morning light
hit them just right
as he relaxed
reading a fine book
in bed

he could pretend they were green

sometimes he thought
that's as good
as it gets

listening to the world

and writing about
what he heard

a decent way
to pass the time

sometimes he surprised himself
the things he heard

in his head
or snatched out of the air

and ordered
in disarray on the page

certainly more interesting
he thought than

what most men did
with their lives

he dreams of a shore

where every stone
is skipping smooth
and the sun
always shines
unless the moon
is smiling

the sand is warm
the crabs are happy
the air lighter than itself
birds dance and dive
to the rhythm
of the sea

where the water
is forty shades of blue
your hand is always there
and when the surf breaks
everything
comes together

today he discovered the age of aches and pains

the age when you're old enough
to feel every little effort

naps are frequent
and sleep is a tossing and turning
of sighs

dreams are mostly temptation
the past dangled in front
like some improbable carrot

it hurts to get out of bed
go to the bathroom
walk to the mailbox
stand in line
wait for the phone to ring
then it even hurts to hear
the phone ringing

headaches backaches
joint pain
stomachaches heartburn toothaches
eye strain rheumatism
neck pain
iron poor blood
and tired swollen sore feet

even though the future looks
more and more
like void
he waits impatiently
for the promise
of his golden years

he knew he could always

get out of his mind
for awhile

choose his poison and take
a vacation

leave this demanding
husk in the dust

swim to the stars
or dance to the beach

listen to waves crash
on billions of miniature mountains

once unconquered peaks
now new oceans

of sand castle ruins
tumbling in a full moon tide

shaping the world
by rubbing against it

over and over and
over again

4

the sunset of the sunset

as all beautiful lumious beings
flood the sky

the oracle does not speak

her tongue tired of lashings
she empties her mind
moves to another sense
rides a silent wave
to your shore

gently knocks on
the ribcage of your home
uses the music of wind whispers
tree moans
floorboard creaks

old refrigerator fans
bubbles secrets in the oatmeal
the high harmonic cry
of the door hinge
chorus of mocking ravens

the improv of screaming lobsters
the low rumble concerto
of heavy weather
the lost rhythm of headboards
the random dance

of a falling fork
loud intervals of cloud quiet
a light switch click
heated counterpoint between fine lines
the lost evidence of spider murder

the discreet cacophony
of butterfly laughter
the bittersweet
rot of carnation decay
the internal pathos of mirrors

the symphony of doorknob rebellions
fugitive keys
and stubborn windows
the sacred songs
of elderly plumbing

no the oracle does not
speak anymore
she swears
by the cold breath
of the moon

halfway around the world

the room spacious
and bright

the bathroom clean
the bed still had a little spring
a fan stood in the corner

there was electricity
sometimes

she stayed behind to read
a modern novel
while he ventured
outside

stuck his head into traffic
picked a direction

followed the flow of sound
and smell
down through the ages

memories inside his code

thousands of years
peeled away

he always liked

the quiet of morning
the air of newborn smell
the calm rain
the sleeping hoards
the parked cars
and silent doorbells

the faint memory
of ring tones
and incessant chatter
gentle waves lapping
at the tongueless
moon

clouds in stealth mode
blossoms tucked in
and all the working birds
in bed dreaming
of tailwinds
and fat worms

that perfect window of peace
between the cracks
of darkness and dawn
twixt the chaos
of bar time
and alarm clocks

when portals yawn
and matter
can pass through the clutter
of thought
to the other side

perpetual dissolve

the days run
into each other

eventually
years collide

and you become
the pieces

someone else tries
to pick up

but now

it avoids humanity
used to lounge on the surface

of everything

cry keep it simple stupid
easy normal uncomplicated
entry level basic

but now
things always get

twisted

layers of extra perception
and desire attached

until nothing is what it seems

only nothing is the most complicated
concept of all

existence looked easy
until the obvious

disappeared

room full of reverb

infinite echoes
and unintelligible
words

perfect for misinterpretation

everybody sounds
underwater
and everything slows

fills the room with haze and cloud
and rain

soon the whole unholy room
is completely underwater

we swim to the windows
but they are painted
closed
so we float to the door but
too much pressure
against it

yet inside the room everything
calm
everything floating
into everything
else

and we understand
it's okay to be afraid afraid

afraid

life is a dream

start and finish
in bed
remember the light
three words and you're done
full of nods and pauses
a few glances
handful of friends
empty glasses dead soldiers
long strong well-defined
legs
walking away
a rhythmic gait
pause
the chase
and a dance or two
only three perfect words
not as many friends
as you think
time work sex fame
death
dozens of shell games
money a bad joke
with a punchline that hits
below the belt
open another bottle
maybe this one has my genie
three perfect words
and you're done
full of nods
and many pauses
into the next

she says she's been waiting

a long time
but no one knows
how long time
really is

yesterday on the news
they said
the universe
will end in 3.7
billion years

then it will collapse
on itself
and start again

that seems like a long time
to a human

but maybe
that's a new york minute
to a universe

just maybe
these are the final hours of everything
and some of us are lucky
enough

to hear the echoes
of the next big bang

the engine of the world

is change

countless moving parts
attracted
and repelled
circling new orbits

spirals of joy and fear

moving into and through
dream matter

in and out of opposites

selfless self
selfish attraction
and reaction
empowering planet anew

into broader
sphere

simple medication

deep power nap
dragon fly cloud
smile from a friend
just ripe banana
smell of a lover
offspring hug
home cooked meal
a listening ear
hot morning shower
cold summer drink
rain on the roof
taste of her lips
toilet that flushes
seawall walk
good night's sleep
dew on dandelions
handy corkscrew
orion's belt
clean clear water
fresh air breath
strong long health
chocolate finish
sunset sunrise
sometimes ordinary
extraordinary
medicine

impermanent pome #942

sky weeps for everyone
clouds own nothing
the wind does not read

these wheels are for spinning
yet sooner or later
the rollercoaster stops

take the mind from the mind
breathe in breath out
calm the calm

third eye meditation

sometimes looking back
is the only way
to move forward
and sometimes moving forward
is the only way
to look back
and sometimes when you
look way out there
you see the back of your head
looking inside for things
unseen yet discovered

remember when we were all water?

perfect charged elastic pure
serene crystal rain
fluid and flowing as the magic stream
in all the ancient stories

we made our own light then
and reflected everything
floated over the timeless dream
splashed away and returned

we tumbled whirled and crashed
without fear or harm
effortlessly bent and reshaped
every landscape

unhurried yet gushing together
running as one
we could drink each other
and only get stronger

borders have blurred

limits fade into memories
your electric fences flooded

lush forests take root
reclaim a new frontier

all gaps close
minds and vistas open

natural bridges appear
ferns vines and herbs reach

for the sky as angels descend
lend a hand lift spirits

even the impossible expanse
between us dissolves

always a self-portrait

every line of the brush
or pen

every warm breath in winter
every stroke of the clock
or hand

we see something we need
to capture

and release

the high lama says

think of everything as
already broken
and one day you won't be
surprised
or disappointed when

the TV goes blank
the vase cracks
your comfortable marriage
unravels

or your very existence
gets caught in a salsa
with death

will you know when it's time
to let go? slip away
from the ritual
into the spiritual
give credit to the stench of life
for a good ride
a fair hearing
a just trial

a kiss that once lasted
eternity

now both lips folded
back

into time

the great wave of dissolve

washes over us
anoints with mortality
and eternity

whispers
you are the sound
of the ocean

the space between mass
the place where vibration
launches itself

make a joyous noise
before your ghost
taps you

on the shoulder
guides you
into another dissolve

elevate your vibration
celebrate the simple
and cyclical

each moment
the great wave of dissolve
washes anew

belugas told me

leave your nets on land
let the fish go
let them grow big again
let families heal themselves

fortunate for you
more air than water
but in the end bad water
will kill us all

dead ocean dead land
try to keep your air clean
try to respect yourself
try to hear our songs to you

we are all of the water
and return to the sky
we are all of the water
and return to the sky

when will your powerful god
teach you
your aquarium is
smaller than you think

the sunset of the sunset

all the world is going down
sinking deeper into
the dark
gluttonous abyss
of the vanishing west

as all beautiful luminous beings
flood the sky
hungry ghosts of every age
crowd defeated
elevators

going down for the last time
faster faster past
the perfect future promised
by quack bankers with cruel blood
on their bills

in distant lands
holy men call this the sunset of the sunset
the magic moment when
all time
is almost gone

my every breath is a prayer for you
my every prayer is a breath of air for you
all my air is every prayer and every prayer for you
my every breath is a prayer for you
my every prayer is a breath of air for you
all my air is every prayer and every prayer for you
my every breath is a prayer for you
my every prayer is a breath of air for you
all my air is every prayer and every prayer for you
my every breath is a prayer for you
my every prayer is a breath of air for you
all my air is every prayer and every prayer for you

breathing mantra

self-portrait in bathroom mirror

Stephen Roxborough (aka roxword) was born in New York to a Canadian father and American mother. He's a past board member for the *Washington Poets Association*, co-founder of *Burning Word* poetry festival, and *Head Poet for Madrona Center* on Guemes Island. An internationally acclaimed, award-winning performance poet, Rox has been twice nominated for the *Pushcart Prize* (2003, 2006), appeared at the *Skagit River Poetry Festival* (2004), *Brave New Words* (Whidbey Island, 2009) and co-edited *radiant danse uv being, a poetic portrait of bill bissett* (2006). He is the author of *making love in the war zone* (2001), *so far all the very long important subversive mind-expanding long ones* (2002), *impeach yourself!* (2006), *blurst* (2009) and *son of blurst* (2010). His spoken word cd, *spiritual demons* (2002) is available at amazon.com and cdbaby.com.

a special word on the typography

erasure *(book title font):*
Eric Oehler was born in Milwaukee and attended the same university as the author (University of Wisconsin, Madison) where he developed a fascination for typography. Oehler based "erasure" on the all-small, sans-serif font used on the cover of early 90s albums by the English synthpop duo of the same name. He currently lives in Madison developing software and fronting his own independent electronica band, Null Device.

Zrnic *(font for author's name):*
Ottawa born Ray Larabie, designed Zrnic based on the original logo for Sony PlayStation. Larabie released over 400 freeware fonts before starting his commercial foundry in 2001 called Typodermic. He now lives in Japan.

Handel Gothic *(poem titles and page numbering font):*
Don Handel created Handel Gothic in the mid-60s to instant success in the graphic design community. It was used in the 1973 United Airlines logo developed by Saul Bass. Handel Gothic became a prominent font in the 80s, primarily used to signify the future. Today's uses include Halo 3, Disney/Pixar film "Wall-E," and recent Star Trek Titles. Handel Gothic's square proportions and a lowercase height that make it an easy-to-read yet still contemporary font

Melior *(poem text font):*
Hermann Zapf, world-renowned master calligrapher and prolific type designer (inventor of over 200 fonts), wanted to create a highly legible typeface ideally suited to newspapers, annual reports, newsletters and a variety of business applications. His result was the straightforward yet elegant Melior. Released in 1952, Melior's strong, square serifs and condensed proportions mimic the superellipse (aka Lame´ curve).

Danish poet/mathematician/scientist/inventor Piet Hein (1905-1996) thought the superellipse was the most beautiful of all forms, and believed it should be used in everything from furniture to city planning. Legend has it that Zapf initially drew the Melior by hand, without knowledge of any mathematical concepts. Years later, Hein pointed out to Zapf his curves were similar to the superellipse construct. Three connected superellipses are used in the logo of the Pittsburgh Steelers.

NeoPoiesis: *a new way of making*

1) in ancient Greece, poiesis referred to the process of making: creation - production - organization - formation - causation

2) a process that can be physical and spiritual, biological and intellectual, artistic and technological, material and teleological, efficient and formal

3) a means of modifying the environment and a method of organizing the self, the making of art and music and poetry, the fashioning of memory and history and philosophy, the construction of perception and expression and reality

4) an independent publisher with a steadfast goal to print and promote outstanding poets, writers and artists that reflect the creative drive and spirit of the new electronic landscape

NeoPoiesisPress.com

www.ingramcontent.com/pod-product-compliance
Lightning Source LLC
LaVergne TN
LVHW091155080426
835509LV00006B/705